T0086526

The Blank Page

STEPHENY BEECHER KENNISON

THE BLANK PAGE

Copyright © 2021 Stepheny Beecher Kennison.

All rights reserved. No part of this book may be used or reproduced by
any means, graphic, electronic, or mechanical, including photocopying,
recording, taping or by any information storage retrieval system
without the written permission of the author except in the case of
brief quotations embodied in critical articles and reviews.

iUniverse books may be ordered through booksellers or by contacting:

iUniverse
1663 Liberty Drive
Bloomington, IN 47403
www.iuniverse.com
844-349-9409

Because of the dynamic nature of the Internet, any web addresses or
links contained in this book may have changed since publication and
may no longer be valid. The views expressed in this work are solely those
of the author and do not necessarily reflect the views of the publisher,
and the publisher hereby disclaims any responsibility for them.

Any people depicted in stock imagery provided by Getty Images are
models, and such images are being used for illustrative purposes only.
Certain stock imagery © Getty Images.

ISBN: 978-1-6632-2631-0 (sc)
ISBN: 978-1-6632-2632-7 (e)

Print information available on the last page.

iUniverse rev. date: 10/27/2021

Stepheny Beecher Kennison

Her gift for writing came from her passion from reading, from learning and from wanting to express herself. She has a Bachelor's in criminal justice from University of Phoenix, she is an Artist, and picked up poetry at a young age. She was raised in Kerrville, Texas but lives in San Angelo with her family and lots of pets. After losing her grandpa she decided writing was her only way to influence others in a positive way. Her mission is to challenge women and men to express themselves in all phases of their lives.

Contents

Life

In life we are on a path
Purely created by our own imagination
There is no right way or wrong way
There is just a destination

Unfold

Unfold her gently
Dissolve her with your words
Press your lips against her skin
Let them liquefy her with your warmth from them
Hold her tight near your chest
Hear her breath calmly
Adore her humbly breath by breath
Unfold her gradually
Learn to accept the parts of her that were left in such agony

Just Be

Be too much
Be a lot
Be breathtaking
Be you
Be anything in this world
Just be you
Be unbelievably astounding
Be weird
Be bizarre
Just be because the world does not want you to

Beneath Her

Beneath her are broken promises
Shattered dreams and cracked walls
She no longer trusts words
They are just lying to get underneath her
To try to see her sorrows
To see if she had an unstable side
They whisper to her with words of such passion
To consume her secrets and to try to break down her walls
But underneath her are emotional breakdowns from
centuries ago
Layers of untouchable sweetness
She is more than being cold hearted
She has been mangled by the words of many
She has fought for herself most of her life
Sometimes she has found herself in nonexistence
So, she goes into a place beneath her
Where only the sunrise can shine
Feeling undervalued and heart wrenching
She would dig deep beneath her to find rays of light
and fire in her eyes
She wanted to feel alive again

She Can

She can do what she wants
Hours and Hours can go by
Just her and her shadow enjoying the fresh air
Sitting by the lake side
Reminiscing the darkest moments of her life
The chains have slowly been broken
She no longer needs to feel needed
She can carry herself without feeling the need to have
a breakthrough
She once was a little girl who was fragile
And has fallen a couple of times
And now she can pick herself up

Ordinary Day

When you let your walls tremble down
You let me have a glance of what's inside
You make me feel as though I do not have to ever look back
My heart shakes unmindfully
When you are not near or close by
It all seems so unreal it makes me wonder, "is this what love is"?
I have not yet to touch you or canoodle you
I do not know what it is to feel you breathing on me
I just know your moods and your smiles
It is just another
Ordinary Day for me

Beach

As the waves hit the shore
Her feet wander beneath the sand
She can feel the sand running through each of her toes
While the waves are playing catch with the sun
She is dancing underneath the clouds and the winds
She made it this far through broken dreams, hurt
relationships and broken friendships
She is still the one she runs to when she is alone and
diddly dallying
She finds herself at the beach where her thoughts and
ideas collide into something bigger other than the
fragments of her life

Stepheny Beecher Kennison

Chocolate Pudding

Every nibble every bite
I feed you with joy in my eyes
Knowing it was your last meal
And our last goodbyes
Your face lit up like a child on the 4th of July

A Space

You demolished every bone within her
She has fallen between the cracks
Completely confused because she does not have you
She feels she is strong, yet she cannot wrap one's mind
around it
Although the wind travels beneath her arms
She tries to be everything you need her to be
She tries to give you every reason to live
She is just a space for you to fill your hatred onto her
A space to empty your misery onto her shoulders
A space for you to take advantage of her most hopeless desires
There is a place in the heart that will never be filled
A space that was stolen a long time ago as a child
A space where love once grew known as cosmic space
A space where she goes and finds solitude
A space of her own existence
A space she can collide into her own self

Accepted

In a world of feelings, she often catches herself in the one
of despair
Each of her bones fills the need to wither away
The pain behind her eyes
The confusion of how certain people perceive her
Her flaws are not beautiful traits anymore
Her flaws are mistakes tolerated
Will the need to find herself accepted end
She seems to put her faith in people and not in God
She loses her way at times
Sometimes it is unthinkable to smile, and it hurts
She wants to feel accepted by people
By individuals who struggle to choose themselves too
Social media is confusing
She often feels the pressure of certain triggers
The triggers in her past come and revisit her often
She has learned to hear her own encouraging words
She prays not for the difficult things in life to go away
She prays for a courage strong enough to overcome the
difficulties in her life

Running Away

Running away is a feeling of rare goosebumps
She wants to save her soul as if it is lost
The tingly feeling from beneath her feet never goes away
The sadness in her eyes is shattering
She prays for the bitterness of those who took her
innocence away
For them to find closure to their mistakes
Because from within this soul is a sad child
She never experienced a genuine love from her mother
She never understood the reasons why she was left out
She will continue to feel the urge of vanishing into her
own loneliness
It is only then when her heart can oddly enough, go on

Soul

It took her years to understand
Why every time she loved she failed
She missed who she wishes she were from another universe
This world is not how she saw it
You see her inner being does not sleep
Her soul stays awake it keeps her up
She finds sleeping difficult because throughout the nights
Even on an empty stomach
More exhausted than before and more alone than ever
Her soul takes her to a place no one knows
Fear not the darkness my sweet soul
For we bloom in the dark before coming into the light
For we grow and blossom into beautiful flowers from the
dirt people
throw at us

Wake me up

She lays awake asleep with her eyes closed
Her heart beating to the echoes of her own breath
She feels insecure in her own bed
She closes her eyes at the end of each sunset
and she falls into a world of her own
Her body has become a prison many times during the nights
Her mind unaware but her physique seemingly asleep
They pull her soul from her
They take her breath away
Her extremities are traumatized from anxiety
Not understanding what they want to hear
She wants to wake up
But she is trembling from below
Someone wake her up if she is motionless
She believes everything she touches shouts out for the souls
of those who crave nourishment
Her nightmares crave her mind as she drifts to sleep
Those special souls crave her touch, and her soul needs
them to keep her moving
She would be the one to weave in and out of your ribs
Searching for a place to keep you protected
So, wake her up and keep her safe and sound
She is not only fighting on earth but in her spiritual visions

What Is Normal

Starving to be normal
She has been in this place before
Its familiar to her the indescribable pain
It is complicated to disburden
She was always looking for a sign of reassurance
They say that happiness will find you, but I think grief
finds you too
The world wants you to be flawless
They want you to be exactly like them
But she is not the same, she is unique, and they
cannot understand
She can feel the fire in someone's heart
She can understand them and hear their silent screams
She can feel the hurt for everyone as if she has known their
energy a life time
As if your souls were once intertwined together
Embracing them is something natural for her
She offers portions of her broken-down spirit to those who
have lost theirs
What is normal? "If she cannot feel normal"?

Break the Silence

We fight every day, but we try our best to love life anyways
So, if you feel you cannot scrape through life
Failing is necessary to survive in life
Failure is such a guilty word for being human
Your journey will not be discovered with just smiles,
laughter, and happy endings
We arrive at the ground at our own feet
Through misfortunes, trials, and disasters
You are only human, and you are allowed to make mistakes
You owe no one an explanation or a reason to why some of
our journeys change directions
Keep pressing forward and break the silence of being perfect
Life is more about learning and losing

Black Sheep

To some she carries the galaxy on her shoulders, and she
walks tall everywhere she goes
To others she was the black sheep of the family
She later realized she was the scapegoat
She was not challenging to love
She was not weird or awkward
She was a rebel at times maybe even a troublemaker
She was just misunderstood and not appreciated
But she never forgot how she was abused by those who
were supposed to love her
There comes a time when turning the page and closing the
book becomes the key to happiness
She learned as she grew older throughout the years from
being an outcast
From being misunderstood most of her life and as a child
Her life was never supposed to be easy nor was it fair
However, the only way to finding harmony was to close the
book and rewrite her story
As many times as she wanted to
Her way on a blank page

Wild Child

She sits there pulling her hair
Constantly thinking of those who tried to destroy her life
Those who took her love for granted
Those who took her kindness for weakness
And although she had a sense of order and a particular style
She was misjudged for being too different
She had an inner wild child within her alive and running free
Everything she touched was meant for good
Her tracs in her fingertips had Gods fingerprints on them
She made many mistakes
Yet God kept blessing her
She knew everything she did good or bad
God would bless her
Her heart was wilder than anyone could see but God himself

Here

Laying next to you broke her soul
Wondering what her life was going to be like without you
She forgot what she was fighting for
She lost herself when she started losing you
She grabbed onto your hand and prayed to not let them
take you
You told her she would be okay here
Placing your hand over her head like a small child
Tapping her gently so you would not hurt her but comfort her
"It is okay you will be okay here" he said
Sometimes I forget how strong I thought I was with you
Until you left here

Jesus and Coffee

She wakes up to start her coffee and to have her little bit
of Jesus
Sometimes she wonders if she will ever make it through
Sometimes she wants to give up and quit the fight
Sometimes the suffering of this world becomes too much
to handle
Sometimes she forgets her faith and then her kids come
running in
As she is drinking her coffee and praying
Her children's smiles make up for everything she is going
through in life
Her kids put the warmth in her coffee
Her kids keep the scriptures alive with in her
Her mistakes in the way she thinks at times
Keep her going back to
Jesus and Coffee

Light

She had a moonstruck smile to hide her pain
She did not want anyone to know she was suffering
from within
She thought about who she could be if she would
expose herself
She was fond of music from Paris, France and music from
El Salvador
Everywhere she went she carried an unusual light
A glimmer, a shine a twinkle or some kind gleam
She always seemed unusually confident
Although deep within her she was controlling certain emotions
She charmed her way through by letting music disperse
through her veins
Music was her way of life it was her joy and her light
from within
If you watched her from a distance, she would tip toe
around with her heavy burdens
But like a glow stick she continues to dance through the
darkness that continues to threaten her radiance

Keep Blessing Her

God will keep blessing her uniqueness
Her kindness is rare
She is unbelievably different yet delicate but bold
She is a ravishing rose when she blooms
But if you disrespect her, she will prick you like a rose
Allow her to bear fruit and she will honor you and
embrace you
She will turn to you like a rebel sunflower would in a field
of wild Sunflowers
Let her shine like a star would through the midnight
night sky
Let her mingle among the galaxies
Because regardless God will keep blessing her
Those who keep throwing stones at her and keep
throwing stones
Will see the works of imperfections into captivating pursuits
She possesses an unwavering love for God
At times she will find herself in a dark place with those stones
And God will continue to bless her
She has known this pattern since she was a small child
But God keeps blessing her through her sorrows
Because she knows evil does not prevail and there will be
another tomorrow

They are Watching

Her walls are closing in as she is running her fingers across
her soul
She knows they are watching, judging, and writing notes on
who she might be
She knows she is not a perfect person but an old soul trying
to unlearn previous behaviors
They have no idea her soul is made from glass,
unmeasurable to the core from within Mother Earth
They think they know her, but they do not know her
They cannot grasp the amount of mistreatment, disrespect
and the lack of care she was raised into
Maybe its human nature we find fault in others by
watching them and characterizing them
Putting people into a little box of quick wittedness
She is nothing like they see her out to be
You cannot determine who she is when she is constantly
evaluating and improving herself from within
She knows they are watching
She knows at times it is more difficult to understand
But her fingertips remind her nothing compares her broken
soul to the one she is reviving

A Sign

As she sits by the riverside listening to the sounds of
the winds
Magical notes whisper into her ears
She ponders about her life as the cricket's chirp near the
field behind her
As she swings on a beautiful shiny green bench
Her heart does not feel as burdensome
As a black grackle watches her from the tallest live oak tree
She seems to be looking for a sign of some kind
She can sense something within her
The feeling of nature being on her side
She has always had a fire within her, but she prefers silence
She does not engage in nonsense fights
She enjoys sitting by the riverside
Seeking for signs because everything comes at the right time

See Me

I hear everything you do not say
You do not need to use words
She was cursed with a mind that never rests and a soul that
never ceases
Her intuition is her superpower
She just wants you to see her
She gravitates towards torn souls
Searching for an eternal place to live
She grew up thinking she was a cursed child
She only shed tears when no one was around
She was like the wilderness waiting for it to rain slightly
Crawl inside her and find the worst of her and see her there
She is just another broken soul searching for meaning in
her life
She yearns to be free of this gift but is haunted by the
what if's
She has endured broken promises and swam with sharks
She just wants you to see her for she is removing her
own heartstrings

Rare

She was the toxic one yet rare in the most magnificent way
a human being could be
She just loved too much and chose to see the world through
her heart
She feels the passion and the grief when she finds herself
close to someone
Her cup overflows with blessing and curses, but she knows
it is never easy to keep herself going
She is a rare stone she is constantly compelled to be
a diamond
But she continues to carry peoples sorrows within
her bones
She is a rare mysterious creature left on earth to find
her soul
She has a fairy tale heart caging her in from being a normal
human being
She knows a beautiful soul when she sees one
Her intuition is her guiding light in her life
She is a rare star she prefers darkness over the light
She knows in her darkest times it has created ultimate
expressions for her inspirations

She is emotionally connected to many
She has a rare gift that holds a heavy-hearted burden
She was born with a rare beauty
Her soul was given to charity at a young age
She wants to fix those she feels passion for
She wanted to heal them
Her beauty was rare it was a mixture of turmoil among the
storm that raged within her

Love is a Shame

She traps herself in the 1960 settings in love with their pure love

She captures herself thinking love is a shame nowadays

She dances in the kitchen alone on her tip toes without help on rainy days

Although if you glance through the window of her small home, she does not look lonesome

She is off alone without a dancer

She is a painter without a paintbrush

She is a writer without words at times

She is a mother without children

Love is a shame sometimes, but she is skin deep in 1960

She thought she would be going to the chapel of love

She knew it would be too good to be true because love only happens in 1960

In the still of her quiet nights, she drifts off to sleep and dreams about being someone's Harlem Girl

She knows we are living in a world of fools

She is stuck in 1960

Wearing bellbottoms, polka dot dresses and scarves with a matching necklace

Stepheny Beecher Kennison

The Seals of her Heart

I can see the ugly in her
Because she has a nasty side of her
Although some of us try to bury it and some of us try to discover it
The seals of her heart are soaked in her own conflicted wounds
Good and evil is within her the battle of right and wrong spins out of control through her bones
She lives by chance and not by choice
Some days she sees people for who they truly are a flicker of light trying to stay lit in a dark place
She knows they are melting and molding again and again
She sees a bit of ugly in people, with their own motives, their own painful past and secrets
She wants to hold their hands through darkness and through their suffering
But the bit of ugly in them makes it impossible because denial is such an ugly trait
She at times wants to escape her body she knows some things in this world she cannot change
The seals of her heart do not make sense, but they are the stories of her ugly parts

Empath

She trusts in people's vibes more than she trusts what they
say or do
Her mind races even when her body is tired
She unconsciously seeks out healing in the healing of others
Although people are drawn to her for healing as if she
carries magic within her veins
She puts everyone's darkness through her
She has become their filter
She has let them in while her light lingered
She feels a complete shift in a person before they can
verbalize it
She is on an endless journey feeling everything or nothing
with no middle ground
Her shadow work is never easy
She is haunted by her demons daily
She tries to acknowledge and find value in herself, but she
finds herself buried
Certain movies make it unbearable for her to watch, the TV
the radio and sometimes the news can drive her crazy
She is highly intuitive, a sensitive old soul with a better
understanding of Mother Earth
She is an emotional creature and naturally a genuine empath

The Emotional Artist

She paints with her shattered soul the music flowing
through her body
The melody dancing through her skin as goosebumps form
on her curvy frame
She is an Emotional Artist capturing her art with her
thoughts, her feelings and tears
She brushes them onto a canvas knowing she just does not
belong here
She was always searching for something from within and
so she became a painter
She is not your typical girl
She is quirky; bohemian, hippish, down to
earth and dances with an unknown spirit
She paints the moon when she feels hollow inside, she feels
radiant underneath the moonlight sky
She is an Emotional Artist if you get too close her essences
will taint you
She will dissolve within you and her penetrating gaze will
capture your conscience

She wants to be unclothed swimming in her feelings while painting with her gypsy soul
She is pure woman she cannot be contain by neither man nor woman
She is her perfect escape, and her beauty is not seen on the outside but from what she carries for others on the inside

Intimacy

She wants to lock eyes with her soulmate
She wants to have a spiritual experience being intimate
with her partner
Breathing one another's energy, connecting and ultimately
discovering it is about understanding one another
She wants to be healed from the inside by gently arousing
her body to release toxins
When her lady flower is being entered her soul is turned on
and a fire has arrived within her
She is wanting to build strength with her love language and
unbelievable boundaries with each touch of her body
Boundaries to a higher consciousness and into a different
mental state
Intimacy is not about performance but about pleasure
She knows she wants her heart to be forever treasured

Spiritual Maintenance

Take those broken wings and learn to fly you were born
into this world with an incredible strong heart
She was planted with a spiritual seed; she has lost her ways
in multiple places and in many ways
She was set up for destruction, raised from ashes and at
times she felt her life was a prison
She took her time to seek him she needed Spiritual
Maintenance to be still
She felt she did not have a chance but the overwhelming
uncontrolled love of God kept chasing her
She grew up knowing his presences, his love and his words
were close
She felt unworthy growing up, unvalued, and she felt
abandoned many times
When she was lost, she rushed to look for herself, but she
found herself in the presences of Gods Spiritual Protection
Although she is unique her constant battle was a need to
conquer herself

So, she waits and wonders if she will be good enough
knowing God would heal her
She will continue to believe in him and in her moments of
spiritual maintenance she will seek him
She will keep finding him
Until he rewrites her story

Enough

She dances to her own music on her tip toes, and she makes
up her own rules along her journey
She is a bit too much for the average person she might not
have diddly squat but she has enough
She expresses herself with the tempo of her spirit and loves
with the depths of her soul
She soaks up the sun with her reckless mind and curvy
frame that is not meant to be tamed
She is a forbidden wild woman she is enough to make your
soul sing
She will shine through you like the sun on a Sunday morning
and make you smile through any chaos you go through
She is enough to be your best friend, your person to run
around with and she will be enough to deepen your smile
She will hold your hand when you are lonely, she will
dance with you in the rain and she will make you feel
more than enough
She is like a sip of sweet whiskey
She will leave her taste on your lips
She will be plenty for you
She is like a midnight sky of unfiltered galaxies
She is a crazy woman but in the most wonderful way most
mysterious this world is well-known for

Ripples

She extends her loving compassion towards others causing
a ripple effect
She creates waves like a surfer on a beach near a sunset
catching her first wave
She admires their struggles
She desires to put their insecurities to sleep
She is a dust storm caused by her strong urges of winds
She wants to catch their tear drops in her hands
She wants to hold their fragile frustrations and break them
free from them
She causes ripple effects like an earthquake
She shakes up their lives for the better, by running her
fingers through their minds
She welcomes them with open arms with their flaws, their
mistakes and their bag of bones
She is their secret keeper, their helper, she is a comforter to
them when they have no one else to turn to
She is like picking up a stone and tossing it into the creek,
where it lands with a satisfying splash
She begins expanding her rings of ripples and slowly they
start to appear
She is a body of water and on the days when you do not feel
any wind there will be some movement in the air through
her ripples

London Bridge

She is like the London bridge watching souls cross the
overpass with nightmares and sweet dreams
She can hear them whisper to themselves that they want to
quit the fight but then they see a flicker of light
She builds London bridges from her heart to theirs
She wants to travel along the twisted trails and experience
the extraordinary worlds of what people have been through
But she knows they will have to take the last few steps on
their own
As we cross our own bridges, we learn to see our successes
and disappointments for greater wisdom
She is a safe place; most can open and unveil their
deepest longings
She will help you feel at ease and relaxed in your most
difficult times
She is strong like the London Bridge she will carry you
through to the other side
For between this world and the Heavens
She knows your soul is not ready to give in
Do not get caught standing in the middle for you might
miss out what is on the other side

Little Human

Little Human spent so much time trying to be perfect
She was a tiny soul withering away alone and brittle
She would lay awake at night without turning off the lights
She was just a little Human trying to just make it in
this world
She came into this world fighting and she has not stop
fighting since
They stole her sweet innocence, took her Birthday wishes
and made her feel useless
She ran with the spirit of the deepest sorrows
forever damaged
Pondering why they would want to strip away her self-
worth layer by layer
She was just a little Human trying to survive in world

Rainy Days

Rainy Days are the days she wants to be happy
Sometimes she finds herself in a sad place and she wants to
carry an umbrella with her
She discovers bits of madness from her emotional
philosophy from what she has been through
Honestly, she wants to drench herself in the storm and have
her painful memories washed away
She has been brutally shattered like a chandelier
A chandelier that once hung from a red dining room that
swung side to side
On those rainy days she can hear thunder pounding away
at the night skies
She can overhear the rain drops crashing below from the
heavy clouds not able to hold them in any longer
On those rainy days she wants to sit in her car a little longer
Listening to music while she drifts away thinking
about nothing
Those rainy days touch her softly
There is a secret language when it rains only a few know
It sounds like waking up to the rain the same way when
rain pours over the earth recklessly

Wild Dancer

Her body soaks up the lyrics of the songs and the melody
runs through her bones
The music pulses through her sensitive parts of her body
She loses herself regardless of what is going on in her life
She is a Wild Dancer
She dances like a flickering flame unable to be defeated
She is her own echo to the sounds of her feet
She moves along the floor with her long muscular legs
The words carrying her soul through the room effortlessly
While feeling the vibrations of her inspirations
She quickly falls into a trance
She is a Wild Dancer
She creates her own beauty with her movements
She is unstoppable
Even her own dancing shadows must catch up to her
She is a Wild Dancer a place she goes to experience magic

Printed in the United States
by Baker & Taylor Publisher Services